never forget a speech!

D0533840

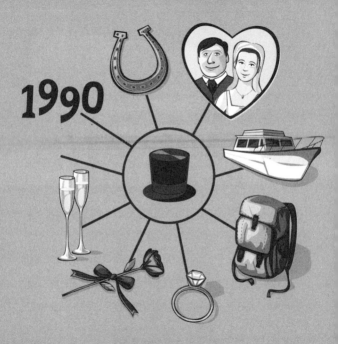

1990

DOMINIC O'BRIEN

never forget a speech!

To anyone terrified at the thought
of public speaking.

Never Forget!
A Speech

Dominic O'Brien

First published in the United
Kingdom and Ircland in 2003 by
Duncan Baird Publishers Ltd
Sixth Floor
Castle House
75–76 Wells Street
London W1T 3QH

Conceived, created and designed
by Duncan Baird Publishers

British Library Cataloguing-in-
Publication Data:
A CIP record for this book is
available from the British Library.

ISBN: 1-904292-50-X

10 9 8 7 6 5 4 3 2 1

Typeset in Helvetica Condensed
Printed and bound in Thailand
by Imago

CONTENTS

MIND MAPS   14

MAKING ASSOCIATIONS   32

THE JOURNEY METHOD   50

THE NUMBER–RHYME SYSTEM   70

THE NUMBER–SHAPE SYSTEM   78

THE DOMINIC SYSTEM   90

PUTTING IT ALL TOGETHER   110

INTRODUCTION

Think back to a speech that really impressed you. The chances are that you found the content interesting, funny or surprising, but above all, I bet the delivery was skilful. I would imagine that rather than reading aloud from a script the orator spoke confidently from memory and addressed the audience directly.

So how do good speakers remember their material so well? You'll be pleased to know that they don't sit down and memorize a speech word for word – or if they do, they're doing it the hard way! The secret of committing a speech to memory is to use a combination of simple techniques ranging from Mind Mapping™ ❯

to visual association. Once you've got the hang of these techniques, you'll be able to apply them effortlessly to any type of speech – whether you're addressing guests at a wedding or a group of delegates at a conference.

As a memory expert, it's essential that I can give talks without even so much as a prompt card. Indeed, it's something that I have come to positively enjoy. I know that soon you'll feel the same way! Speech-giving will cease to be a nerve-wracking experience and will become a skill that you're proud to show off.

Dominic O'Brien

SYMBOLS USED IN THIS BOOK

🔧 MEMORY TECHNIQUE

✔ MEMORY IN ACTION

💡 MEMORY WISDOM

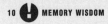

KNOW YOUR MATERIAL

People often think that they have to learn a speech off by heart. This isn't so. A speech that is recited word for word can sound stilted and unnatural. The more impressive speaker understands that it is far better to know the content of the material so well that you can just talk about it confidently and spontaneously. >

Don't worry if this sounds daunting – I'm going to show you a variety of techniques to help you remember the content and order of your speech so that you will feel entirely confident about a non-rote delivery. Of course, there are some aspects of a speech, such as names, figures and dates, that you do need to memorize in a very precise way, and I'll explain how to do this too.

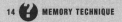

MIND MAPS

Many people rely on numerous pieces of paper covered in notes when they make a speech. Imagine how much simpler it would be to have a single sheet of paper that shows your speech in the form of a diagram. This is where Mind Maps come in. Mind Maps were invented by Tony Buzan who has written or co-authored 82 bestselling books. ❯

It's easy to make a Mind Map. First, draw an image that represents the subject of your speech in the middle of a piece of paper. Next, think of all the core points or themes of your speech – draw a branch (each with its own colour) emanating from the central image for each topic. Label each branch with a symbol or key word. Sub-topics can form sub-branches.

HERE'S HOW IT WORKS.

IMAGINE THAT YOU ARE A BEST MAN GIVING A SPEECH AT A WEDDING. YOUR MIND MAP SHOULD START WITH THE NAMES OF THE BRIDE AND GROOM (LET'S SAY THEY ARE CALLED LEAH AND MARK). PUT THE NAMES IN THE CENTRE OF A BLANK PAGE. NOW BRAINSTORM THE MAIN POINTS THAT YOU NEED TO RAISE IN YOUR SPEECH — FOR EXAMPLE, WHERE YOU MET

THE GROOM; KIND THINGS ABOUT THE BRIDE; THANKS AND TOASTS TO PARENTS/BRIDESMAIDS AND SO ON. DRAW A BRANCH FOR EACH TOPIC. REMEMBER TO LABEL THE BRANCHES WITH JUST ONE KEY WORD ("COLLEGE"; "LEAH"; "TOAST") OR WITH AN IMAGE. IF AN IDEA COMES TO YOU THAT IS RELATED TO ONE OF THE MAIN TOPICS BUT IS NOT A MAIN TOPIC IN ITSELF, DRAW A SUB-BRANCH AND LABEL IT. DON'T TRY TO EDIT YOUR IDEAS AT THIS STAGE, JUST LET THEM FLOW — KEEP ADDING BRANCHES AND SUB-BRANCHES.

THE FIRST MIND MAP YOU PRODUCE WILL PROBABLY BE AN ELABORATE ONE WITH MULTIPLE BRANCHES, SUB-BRANCHES AND EVEN SUB-SUB-BRANCHES. IF YOUR MIND MAP LOOKS CONFUSING, IT'S WORTH DRAWING A SECOND MAP. THIS TIME EDIT OUT THE POINTS THAT APPEAR LEAST RELEVANT AND CONDENSE RELATED IDEAS INTO A FEW CORE POINTS. ❯

Remember — your Mind Map should be a simple visual guide to the main parts of your speech. If you need to spend more than a few seconds scrutinizing the map in order to make sense of it, it will defeat its purpose.

Be sure to choose one word only, or an image, rather than writing intricate notes around each branch. I'm going to give you some examples of how I would label the branches of my Leah and Mark Mind Map.

• Main branch colour: Green — key word: "College" This reminds me to speak about how I first met Mark at college. A sub-branch with the date "1990" tells me that I met him in that year. A sub-sub-branch labelled "first" reminds me to mention that — to everyone's surprise — Mark

1990

MANAGED TO BAG HIMSELF A FIRST CLASS HONOURS!

A SUB-BRANCH KEY IMAGE ON THE LEAH BRANCH MIGHT BE A LUCKY CHARM. THIS REMINDS ME TO TALK ABOUT HOW LUCKY MARK HAS ALWAYS BEEN. HE ALWAYS SEEMED TO FALL ON HIS FEET IN LIFE, INCLUDING DATING THE BEST LOOKING GIRL IN COLLEGE — THE BEAUTIFUL BRIDE HERSELF, LEAH. >

• **MAIN BRANCH COLOUR: BLUE – KEY WORD: "COUPLE"**
THIS PROMPTS ME TO TALK ABOUT MARK AND LEAH AS A
COUPLE. THERE'S A JOKE I WANT TO GET IN HERE AND, TO
REMIND MYSELF OF THIS, I DRAW A SMILEY FACE BESIDE
THE WORD "COUPLE".

I DRAW AN IMAGE OF A BOAT ON A SUB-BRANCH. THIS
REMINDS ME TO RELATE A FUNNY ANECDOTE ABOUT A

BOATING HOLIDAY THAT I WENT ON WITH MARK, LEAH AND SOME OTHER FRIENDS SHORTLY AFTER THEY STARTED GOING OUT TOGETHER.

THE COUPLE BRANCH MIGHT ALSO HAVE A SUB-BRANCH LABELLED WITH A BACKPACK. THIS REMINDS ME TO TALK ABOUT HOW LEAH AND MARK TOOK SIX MONTHS OUT TO GO TRAVELLING ROUND SOUTHEAST ASIA TOGETHER.

A SUB-SUB-BRANCH KEY WORD MIGHT BE "PROPOSAL". THIS REMINDS ME TO SAY THAT MARK PROPOSED TO LEAH ON THE PLANE ON THE WAY HOME FROM THEIR TRAVELS. >

A THIRD SUB-BRANCH KEY WORD ON THE COUPLE BRANCH MIGHT BE "ROMANTIC" OR I MIGHT DRAW AN IMAGE OF A ROSE (STILL IN THE COLOUR BLUE). THIS REMINDS ME TO TALK ABOUT HOW ROMANTIC MARK AND LEAH ARE WITH EACH OTHER AND HOW THEY ARE "MADE FOR EACH OTHER".

"ROMANTIC"

• **MAIN BRANCH COLOUR: RED – KEY WORD: "TOAST"**
THIS REMINDS ME TO TOAST ALL THE WEDDING GUESTS. A SUB-BRANCH LABELLED "THANKS" REMINDS ME TO THANK SPECIFIC PEOPLE, SUCH AS BRIDESMAIDS AND CATERERS (I CAN LIST THE NAMES ON SUB-SUB-BRANCHES).

I LABEL ANOTHER SUB-BRANCH WITH TWO MATCHSTICK PEOPLE. THIS REMINDS ME TO MAKE A FINAL TOAST TO THE BRIDE AND GROOM. AND A SUB-SUB-BRANCH LABELLED "FUTURE" TELLS ME TO SAY "BEST WISHES FOR THE FUTURE". ›

OF COURSE, IT'S MORE DIFFICULT TO DESCRIBE A MIND MAP IN WORDS THAN IT IS ACTUALLY TO DRAW ONE. MY MIND MAP OF THE MARK AND LEAH SPEECH WOULD CONSIST OF FOUR MAIN BRANCHES, EIGHT SUB-BRANCHES AND SIX SUB-SUB BRANCHES. IT MIGHT LOOK SOMETHING LIKE THE ONE SHOWN OPPOSITE.

IT MAY BE USEFUL TO IMPOSE A SEQUENCE ON THE IDEAS IN MY MIND MAP. BEFORE YOU DRAW YOUR REFINED VERSION OF THE MIND MAP DECIDE WHETHER YOU WANT TO READ THE MAP CLOCKWISE FROM 12 O'CLOCK OR ANTICLOCKWISE, AND POSITION YOUR BRANCHES IN THE RIGHT ORDER ACCORDING TO THE SYSTEM YOU CHOOSE.

first 1990

Beautiful

A Mind Map containing a group of key words and images will provide you with a superb memory prompt – and you won't be burdened with odd bits of paper that might get out of order. You now have a choice. You can either take your Mind Map along to your speech and glance at it whenever you need to or you can commit the key words to memory and deliver a paper-free speech on the day!

I'd encourage you to go the latter route. It may sound intimidating, but there's no need for you to be alarmed – later I'm going to teach you some excellent techniques for memorizing key words, and then I'm going to show you how to embed them in your memory in the right order. Once you've got the hang of all the techniques, you'll be confident enough for a completely paper-free speech.

COLOURS AND SYMBOLS

Our brains are stimulated by things that are visually striking. Make your Mind Map as eye-catching as possible. Draw the main branches in different colours and add images wherever you can. In a wedding speech you could draw a big diamond engagement ring to remind you to talk about a proposals.

MAKING ASSOCIATIONS

When I want to memorize key words for a speech, I like to give each key word an imaginative association in my mind – this way the word (and its relevance) is easier to recall. "Imaginative" is an important word here – I don't remember a beach ball by conjuring up the words "spherical object, typically made of plastic and filled with air". ❯

I think of something brightly coloured and thrown about on a beautiful sandy beach; I visualize ice-cream sellers and clear blue water, and I imagine the sun beating down on my back. This makes the image of a beach ball much more memorable! The art of association can give things that are abstract a set of personal characteristics that are easily and instantly memorable. >

Think back to your Mind Map of the wedding speech. How might you remember that one of the main branch key words is "Toast"? If you picture the Mind Map in your head, you might imagine that in the top left corner of it, corks are popping and people are cheering. Perhaps confetti is raining down. You see! As soon as the word or phrase comes alive, it becomes more memorable. Remember – try not to rely on anyone else's ideas, your own associations are the best ones because they are personal and they will stick.

TOAST

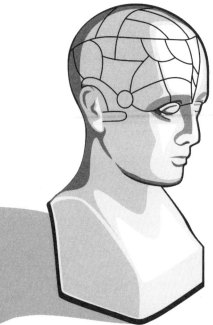

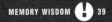

USE FREE ASSOCIATION

The psychoanalyst Sigmund Freud used free association as a means of exploring the unconscious. He encouraged his patients to express their subconscious thoughts – to free their minds and to simply say the first thing that came into their heads. Clear your mind and make way for intuitive and instantaneous thinking.

HERE'S AN EXAMPLE OF HOW ASSOCIATION CAN HELP BRING MIND MAPS TO LIFE AND MAKE A SPEECH MORE MEMORABLE. IMAGINE THAT YOU HAVE TO GIVE A TALK TO YOUR MANAGERS ABOUT THE ANNUAL PERFORMANCE OF YOUR TEAM. YOU'VE MIND-MAPPED YOUR TALK AND YOU'VE COME UP WITH THESE KEY WORDS:

Profits
Absenteeism
Streamlining
Training
Budgets
Advertising

THESE KEY WORDS ARE ALL QUITE UNINTERESTING — THEY DON'T AUTOMATICALLY FIRE THE IMAGINATION OR FILL US WITH ENTHUSIASM. THIS IS WHY I'D LIKE YOU TO SPEND A FEW MINUTES FORMING ASSOCIATIONS FOR THESE WORDS — IF YOU CAN FREE ASSOCIATE WITH UNINSPIRING WORDS YOU CAN FREE ASSOCIATE WITH ANYTHING! YOU NEED TO COME UP WITH STRONG IMAGES THAT WILL IMMEDIATELY REMIND YOU OF THE KEY WORD. HOW YOU COME UP WITH AN ASSOCIATION DOESN'T REALLY MATTER. AN IMAGE MIGHT JUST POP UNSOLICITED INTO YOUR HEAD, OR THE KEY WORD MIGHT SOUND LIKE OR RHYME WITH ANOTHER WORD. THE IMPORTANT THING IS THAT THE ASSOCIATIONS YOU FORM HAVE STRONG PERSONAL RESONANCE FOR YOU. >

HERE ARE MY ASSOCIATIONS.

PROFITS – A BLACK, LEATHER BRIEFCASE PACKED TIGHTLY WITH WADS OF DOLLAR BILLS.

ABSENTEEISM – A CARTOON DRAWING OF A MAN LYING IN BED IN HIS PYJAMAS WITH A THERMOMETER IN HIS MOUTH, RED SPOTS ALL OVER HIS FACE AND HIS ARM IN A SLING.

STREAMLINING – A MAN TRYING TO WALK IN A STRAIGHT LINE UP A FAST MOVING STREAM.

TRAINING – A GROUP OF STUDENT DOCTORS STANDING AT THE BED OF A HOSPITAL PATIENT AND TAKING NOTES.

BUDGETS — A VERY SMALL MAN SAYING "BUDGE IT" TO AN INCREDIBLY LARGE MAN BLOCKING HIS PATH.

ADVERTISING — AN ENORMOUS WHITE BILLBOARD ON A CITY STREET.

YOU'LL NOTICE THAT I'VE EMBELLISHED SOME OF MY IMAGES WITH SPECIFIC VISUAL DETAIL. FOR EXAMPLE, MY ASSOCIATION WITH THE KEY WORD "PROFIT" IS NOT JUST DOLLAR BILLS BUT WADS OF DOLLAR BILLS WHICH ARE PACKED TIGHTLY IN A BLACK LEATHER BRIEFCASE. THESE DETAILS HELP TO BRING THE IMAGE ALIVE FOR ME. IF YOU HAVE TROUBLE REMEMBERING YOUR KEY WORDS, I SUGGEST THAT YOU ENRICH YOUR ASSOCIATIONS WITH MORE LAVISH VISUAL DETAIL. MAKE THEM BIGGER, BRIGHTER AND BOLDER — THE MORE COMICAL, ECCENTRIC OR LARGER THAN LIFE AN IMAGE IS, THE EASIER IT IS TO REMEMBER.

BEFORE WE MOVE ON TO OTHER WAYS IN WHICH ASSOCIATION CAN BE USEFUL IN SPEECH-GIVING, IT'S WORTH LOOKING AT HOW YOU CAN USE ASSOCIATION TO REMEMBER PEOPLE'S NAMES. NAMES FEATURE LARGELY IN ALL TYPES OF PRESENTATION, FROM A HISTORY LECTURE TO A SPEECH AT A COLLEGE REUNION, AND EVEN A JOB INTERVIEW. I'D LIKE YOU TO IMAGINE FOR A MOMENT THAT YOU ARE THE COACH OF A COLLEGE SPORTS TEAM AND YOU ARE GIVING OUT PRIZES AT YOUR ANNUAL SPORTS DAY. THE FOLLOWING PEOPLE WILL BE COLLECTING PRIZES AND YOU NEED TO COMMIT THEIR NAMES TO MEMORY:

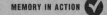

Gemma Marshall
Angela Wallace
Jack Walker
Warren Bailey
Robert Willis

TAKE A LOOK AT THE WAY I'D DO IT. IN THE CASE OF
GEMMA MARSHALL, I IMAGINE A WOMAN DRIPPING WITH
GEM STONES IN THE FORM OF NECKLACES, PENDANTS
AND BRACELETS. SHE HAS A DISTINCTIVE MARSHALL'S
BADGE THAT IS DECORATED WITH DIAMONDS ON THE LAPEL
OF HER JACKET.

I COMMIT ANGELA WALLACE TO MEMORY BY VISUALIZING
AN ANGEL FLYING THROUGH A WALL OF LACE. >

JACK WALKER BECOMES
MEMORABLE IF I PICTURE A
CHILDREN'S NURSERY. AS I ENTER
A JACK-IN-THE-BOX SPRINGS UP
AND I'M SO SURPRISED I STUMBLE
OVER A CHILD'S WALKER.

WARREN BAILEY MAKES ME THINK
OF A FIELD FULL OF RABBIT HOLES
LEADING TO A BIG UNDERGROUND
WARREN. THERE IS A BAY TREE IN
THE CORNER OF THE FIELD SHEDDING
BAY LEAVES.

ROBERT WILLIS REMINDS ME OF **ROBERT DE NIRO** AND BRUCE **WILLIS**. I IMAGINE THEM BOTH TRYING TO BE FIRST TO SHAKE MY HAND. ROBERT DE NIRO IS FIRST BECAUSE HE COMMANDS BRUCE WILLIS TO STAND BEHIND HIM (THIS IS TO REMIND ME THAT I TAKE ROBERT DE NIRO'S FIRST NAME AND BRUCE WILLIS'S LAST NAME).

YOU'LL NOTICE THAT I'VE CREATED LITTLE STORIES WITH SOME OF MY ASSOCIATIONS. STORIES ARE NATURALLY ENGAGING AND MEMORABLE, AND IF THEY'RE SLIGHTLY STRANGE OR QUIRKY WE REMEMBER THEM ALL THE BETTER.

BREAK IT DOWN

If you find it difficult to form an association with a particular word, break it down into its component syllables and form a series of associations instead. This technique can be called "part-wording". It's especially useful for foreign names that don't mean much to you in their entirety.

THE JOURNEY METHOD

We have looked at two of the three keys to memory – imagination and association. Now it's time to turn to the third key – location. We often talk about being able to "place" something when we try to recall it. With the Journey Method everything you want to remember is placed. You think of the place and you remember the item. Easy! >

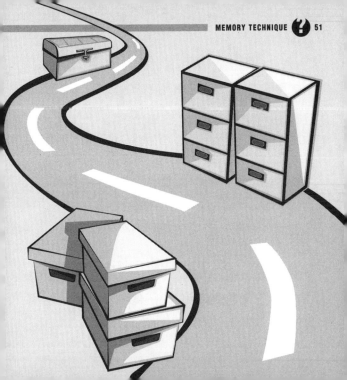

Here's how it works. First you think of a journey that you know well – for example, your drive to work. Then you identify points along the route that can act as "storage places" for the things that you want to remember.

When you come to store the items to memorize them, you mentally make the journey. As you come to each stage, you place an item there – using as much vivid association as you can to make the link between the place and the item as bold and memorable as possible. Later, when you need to recapture what you've memorized, you mentally make the journey again and as you reach each stage, the association should automatically spring to mind – along with the thing that you need to recall.

LET'S IMAGINE THAT YOU ARE A WELL-KNOWN ROMANTIC NOVELIST AND YOU HAVE BEEN INVITED TO GIVE A TALK TO A GROUP OF ASPIRING WRITERS ABOUT THE DO'S AND DON'TS OF ROMANTIC FICTION WRITING.

FIRST, YOU BRAINSTORM ALL YOUR IDEAS AND PRODUCE A MIND MAP. HERE ARE THE MAIN IDEAS THAT YOU WISH TO SHARE WITH YOUR AUDIENCE AND THE KEY WORDS THAT REPRESENT EACH IDEA.

• IDEA: DO CREATE A BELIEVABLE PLOT WITH A DEFINITE STARTING POINT, A MIDDLE AND A CONCLUSION. ROMANTIC FICTION SHOULDN'T JUST CONSIST OF A SEQUENCE OF LOOSELY RELATED LOVE SCENES.

KEY WORD: "PLOT"

• **IDEA: DO USE SUSPENSE. KEEP THE READER GUESSING ABOUT WHAT HAPPENS NEXT. INTRODUCE CRISES, COMPLICATIONS AND CONFLICTS AND DON'T RESOLVE THEM STRAIGHT AWAY.**
KEY WORD: "SUSPENSE"

• **IDEA: DO CREATE BELIEVABLE CHARACTERS WHOM THE READER WILL RELATE TO. MAKE THE CHARACTERS TAKE AN EMOTIONAL JOURNEY THAT CHALLENGES THEM IN SOME WAY.**
KEY WORD: "CHARACTER"

• **IDEA: DO WRITE PLAUSIBLE DIALOGUE IN WHICH CHARACTERS SAY MEANINGFUL AND INTERESTING THINGS WITH WIT AND ENERGY.**
KEY WORD: "DIALOGUE" >

- **IDEA:** DO MAKE SURE YOU HAVE A HAPPY ENDING. READERS OF ROMANTIC FICTION TEND TO DISLIKE GRITTY OR PESSIMISTIC OUTCOMES.
KEY WORD: "HAPPY"

- **IDEA:** DON'T INTRODUCE LOVE SCENES TOO EARLY. ALLOW THE ROMANTIC TENSION TO BUILD UP FIRST.
KEY WORD: "TENSION"

- **IDEA:** DON'T BE CORNY AND DON'T WRITE IN CLICHÉS, SUCH AS "SHE MOANED AND FELL INTO HIS ARMS".
KEY WORD: "CORNY"

- **IDEA:** DON'T BE INHIBITED WHEN YOU WRITE LOVE SCENES — IF YOU HAVE HANG-UPS IT WILL SHOW IN YOUR WRITING.
KEY WORD: "HANG-UPS"

• **IDEA: DON'T BE TOO SENTIMENTAL OR TRITE. YOUR READERS WANT TO RELATE TO OR FALL IN LOVE WITH THE CHARACTERS — THEY DON'T WANT TO FEEL PATRONIZED. KEY WORD: "SENTIMENTAL"**

• **IDEA: DON'T WRITE CLINICAL OR EXPLICIT LOVE SCENES. YOUR READERS WANT A ROMANTIC AND SENSUAL BUZZ — NOT AN ANATOMY LESSON. KEY WORD: "CLINICAL" >**

NOW YOU NEED TO DO SOME FREE ASSOCIATION TO PAIR YOUR KEY WORDS WITH STRONG VISUAL SYMBOLS. HERE'S A LIST OF ASSOCIATIONS THAT I'VE COME UP WITH. THESE ARE UNIQUE TO ME — YOU SHOULD TRY TO COME UP WITH YOUR OWN WHICH WILL BE PERSONAL AND MORE MEMORABLE TO YOU.

Plot – A PLOT OF LAND WAITING FOR A HOUSE TO BE BUILT ON IT

Suspense – A SUSPENSION BRIDGE

Character – A CHARACTER ACTRESS DRESSED IN ELIZABETHAN COSTUME

Dialogue – A PERSON DYING ON A LOG

Happy – A SMILING BABY

Tension – A MAN SITTING AT A DESK, HEAD IN HANDS

Corny – A FIELD OF CORN

Hang-up – A CLOTHES HANGER

Sentimental – A BIG RED, INFLATABLE HEART

Clinical – A DOCTOR

YOU'LL NOTICE THAT ALL MY ASSOCIATIONS ARE NOUNS – THIS IS DELIBERATE. NOUNS ARE MEMORABLE BECAUSE THEY'RE EASY TO VISUALIZE. AS A RULE, IT'S MUCH MORE DIFFICULT TO PICTURE VERBS OR ADJECTIVES.

THE NEXT STAGE IS TO STORE YOUR VISUAL SYMBOLS ALONG A JOURNEY THAT IS FAMILIAR TO YOU. SO PICK A JOURNEY THAT YOU KNOW VERY WELL AND IDENTIFY 10 LANDMARKS ALONG THE ROUTE (ONE FOR EACH IDEA THAT YOU WANT TO DISCUSS IN YOUR SPEECH). THE LANDMARKS THAT YOU CHOOSE MUST BE STATIONARY

— THEY ARE FIXED. THE EXAMPLE THAT I'M GOING TO USE IS THE WALK FROM MY HOME TO THE TRAIN STATION.

THE 10 LANDMARKS THAT ARE MOST FAMILIAR TO ME ALONG THIS WALK ARE A HOUSE WITH BOARDED UP WINDOWS, A PEDESTRIAN CROSSING ON A BUSY STREET THAT IS ALWAYS DIFFICULT TO CROSS, A FISH POND, A FALLEN TREE, A CANDY STORE, A PHOTOCOPYING BUREAU, A TRAVEL AGENT, SOME RECYCLING BINS, THE STEPS LEADING TO THE STATION AND, FINALLY, THE TICKET OFFICE.

NOW I'M GOING TO SHOW YOU HOW TO STORE THE VISUAL SYMBOLS FOR THE ROMANTIC NOVEL-WRITING SPEECH IN EACH OF THESE LANDMARKS. YOU SHOULD TRY TO DO THE SAME WITH YOUR OWN ASSOCIATIONS AND YOUR OWN JOURNEY. ❯

I MENTALLY BEGIN MY WALK TO THE TRAIN STATION. THE FIRST LANDMARK I COME ACROSS IS THE BOARDED UP HOUSE. I'VE LONG THOUGHT THAT IT'S TIME THAT SOMEONE KNOCKED THIS DOWN AND BUILT SOMETHING NEW SO IT'S EASY FOR ME TO VISUALIZE A BARE PLOT OF LAND HERE. THIS WILL REMIND ME TO TALK ABOUT PLOT.

NOW I COME TO THE PEDESTRIAN CROSSING ON THE BUSY STREET. AMAZINGLY, AS I STEP ONTO THE ROAD, THE CROSSING TURNS INTO A SUSPENSION BRIDGE WHICH ALLOWS ME TO CROSS QUICKLY, SAFELY AND EASILY AND DOESN'T HOLD UP THE TRAFFIC. THIS WILL REMIND ME TO TALK ABOUT SUSPENSE.

I REACH MY NEXT LANDMARK — THE FISH POND. IT'S HARDER TO MAKE THE CONNECTION HERE, SO I USE MY SENSES AND IMAGINATION — I IMAGINE AN ELEGANT

ELIZABETHAN LADY TRIPPING OVER HER HUGE DRESS AND
FALLING INTO THE POND. SHE BEGINS SCREAMING AND
SPLASHING ABOUT AND USES HER PARASOL TO TRY TO
PULL HERSELF TO THE EDGE. FISH BEGIN LEAPING OUT
OF THE POND IN FEAR. THIS WILL REMIND ME TO TALK
ABOUT CHARACTER. >

NEXT I COME TO THE FALLEN TREE. THIS ASSOCIATION IS EASY — I VISUALIZE A PERSON DRAPED OVER THE TRUNK OF THE TREE MOANING IN THE THROES OF DRAMATIC DEATH. THIS REMINDS ME TO TALK ABOUT DIALOGUE.

NEXT I COME TO THE CANDY STORE. I SEE IT FILLED, FLOOR TO CEILING, WITH SMILING JELLY BABIES — THERE ARE THOUSANDS OF THEM IN ALL DIFFERENT COLOURS. THIS REMINDS ME TO TALK ABOUT A HAPPY ENDING.

WHEN I REACH THE PHOTOCOPYING BUREAU, I SEE A QUEUE OF MEN SEATED OUTSIDE WAITING TO USE THE PHOTOCOPIERS. THEY ALL HAVE THEIR HEADS IN THEIR HANDS AND LOOK REALLY STRESSED OUT. THIS REMINDS ME TO TALK ABOUT THE IMPORTANCE OF TENSION IN THE STORY.

THEN I COME TO THE TRAVEL AGENT. HERE, THE WINDOW IS FILLED WITH POSTERS OF A PLACE BRIMMING WITH GOLDEN FIELDS OF CORN — PERHAPS THERE IS AN IMAGE OF A MAN AND A WOMAN RUNNING THROUGH THE FIELDS. IT'S ADVERTISING ROMANTIC HONEYMOONS. THIS REMINDS ME THAT STORIES SHOULDN'T BE CORNY! >

NEXT ARE THE RECYCLING BINS. SOME OF THE BINS ARE FOR CLOTHES AND I IMAGINE THAT, AS WELL AS THEIR OLD GARMENTS, SOMEONE HAS DUMPED AN ENTIRE EMPTY WARDROBE NEXT TO THE BINS, WITH ITS DOORS SLAMMING IN THE WIND. THIS WILL REMIND ME TO TALK ABOUT HANG-UPS.

AS I JOG UP THE STEPS TO THE STATION (SOMETHING THAT RAISES MY HEART RATE), I IMAGINE THAT SOMEONE HAS TIED A BIG, RED, INFLATABLE HEART TO THE HANDRAIL. THIS WILL REMIND ME TO TALK ABOUT SENTIMENTALITY.

FINALLY, I GET TO THE TICKET OFFICE. I IMAGINE THAT INSTEAD OF A TICKET SELLER THE MAN BEHIND THE GLASS IS A DOCTOR WEARING A WHITE COAT AND A STETHOSCOPE AND HE WANTS TO LISTEN TO MY HEART (THIS CONVENIENTLY TIES IN IN WITH MY LAST VISUAL IMAGE). THIS WILL REMIND ME TO TALK ABOUT CLINICAL DESCRIPTIONS.

NOW I'VE STORED ALL MY VISUAL IMAGES AT POINTS ALONG MY ROUTE I WILL COMPLETE MY JOURNEY SEVERAL MORE TIMES IN MY HEAD JUST TO MAKE SURE THAT I KNOW WHERE EVERYTHING IS. YOU SHOULD DO THE SAME. NOW PRACTISE THE ROMANTIC NOVEL-WRITING SPEECH USING THE JOURNEY METHOD AS YOUR ONLY PROP.

PLEASANT JOURNEYS

When you use the Journey Method to memorize a speech it can help to choose a journey that is relevant to your subject. For example, the walk to a local church for a wedding speech. Or, if you feel uninspired by the subject matter, choose a journey that has happy or amusing associations to help inspire you.

THE NUMBER–RHYME SYSTEM

Speeches often contain numbers. Sometimes you just need to remember one or two dates. Other times you need to reel off an extensive list of figures – for example, in a sales presentation. People tend to find numbers daunting to memorize because they are abstract. In order to remember them, we need to make them interesting. ❯

The Number–Rhyme technique is popular among magicians for remembering sequences of numbers. It works on the principle that words and images are more memorable than numbers. You need to think of a word that rhymes with each number from 0 to 9. You should learn your rhymes so well that every time you see the number four, say, an image of a door pops into your head. These are the rhymes that I use most frequently. You don't have to use my rhymes – they're just suggestions.

0 – A HERO
1 – A BUN, A NUN OR THE SUN
2 – A SHOE OR SOME GLUE
3 – A TREE, A BEE OR A KNEE
4 – A DOOR, A SAW OR A PAW
5 – A HIVE OR A DIVE
6 – SOME STICKS OR SOME BRICKS
7 – HEAVEN
8 – A GATE, A DATE OR A WEIGHT
9 – SOME WINE, A LINE OR A SIGN

LET'S LOOK AT THE NUMBER–
RHYME TECHNIQUE IN ACTION.

IMAGINE THAT YOU ARE A
TEACHER SHOWING PROSPECTIVE
PARENTS AROUND A SCHOOL AND
YOU WANT TO MENTION PAST
ACADEMIC PERFORMANCE.
USING THE NUMBER–RHYME
SYSTEM, HOW WOULD YOU
REMEMBER THAT THE PASS
RATES FOR ENGLISH,
MATHEMATICS AND HISTORY ARE
83%, 70% AND 92%
RESPECTIVELY?
HERE'S HOW YOU MIGHT HAVE
DONE IT:

TO REMEMBER "83" YOU COULD IMAGINE A DATE TREE. TO TIE THIS INTO THE SUBJECT OF ENGLISH YOU COULD IMAGINE WRITING A POEM ABOUT A DATE TREE.

TO REMEMBER "70" YOU COULD IMAGINE BEING IN HEAVEN AND MEETING YOUR GREATEST HERO. TO TIE THIS INTO THE SUBJECT OF MATHEMATICS YOUR HERO COULD BE PYTHAGORAS.

TO REMEMBER "92" IMAGINE MAKING A SIGN AND STICKING IT UP WITH SOME GLUE. TO TIE THIS INTO THE SUBJECT OF HISTORY, THE SIGN COULD READ: "HISTORY LESSONS THIS WAY."

AS WITH MANY MEMORY TECHNIQUES, BY TURNING YOUR ASSOCIATIONS INTO A LITTLE STORY OR SCENE, YOU ARE ABLE TO EMBED THEM MORE FIRMLY IN YOUR MIND.

TAKE-AWAY FIGURES

If you have a job in sales or finance, or if you are responsible for a team's performance, the chances are that you will have to make many speeches involving figures. Impress your colleagues by presenting from memory, but be ready with handouts for them to take away – they may not have your impressive skills of recall!

THE NUMBER–SHAPE SYSTEM

If you think visually, as I do, you might find that the Number–Rhyme system doesn't work so well for you. Instead, try turning numbers into shapes to make them more memorable. The Number–Shape system looks at the shape of the digit and links that shape to an object that has a similar form. You can see how it works on the following pages. >

To use the Number–Shape system, begin by pairing each number from zero to nine with an image that resembles the digit in terms of shape or outline. You can be as imaginative as you like. Here are my ideas, but feel free to invent your own:

0 — ANYTHING ROUND, SUCH AS A BALL OR A RING

1 — ANYTHING STRAIGHT AND VERTICAL, SUCH AS A CANDLE, A PENCIL OR A ROCKET

2 — A SWAN, OR A SNAKE ABOUT TO STRIKE

3 — A PAIR OF PUCKERED LIPS

4 — A FLAG ON A FLAG POLE OR AN UNFURLED SAIL ON A YACHT

5 — A SEAHORSE OR AN S-SHAPED HOOK

6 — AN ELEPHANT'S TRUNK OR A GOLF CLUB

7 — A BOOMERANG OR THE EDGE OF A CLIFF

8 — A SNOWMAN OR AN HOURGLASS

9 — A BALLOON ON A RIBBON OR A MONOCLE ›

Rehearse your number–shapes in your head a few times until you feel confident about remembering the associations – the aim is to be able to translate one to the other and back again in an instant. This exercise will help you: read through the rows of numbers shown opposite from left to right, translating them into shapes as you go. Keep practising until you can do it very quickly.

5	7	3	1	0
2	4	7	9	5
6	8	0	2	7
1	3	4	9	1
8	2	5	0	6

Once you are confident that your associations are firmly embedded in your mind, you are ready to put number–shapes into practice.

IMAGE THAT YOU BELONG TO A MOVIE APPRECIATION SOCIETY AND YOU'RE GIVING A TALK ABOUT YOUR FAVOURITE THREE STEVEN SPIELBERG MOVIES. YOU NEED TO REMEMBER THE YEARS IN WHICH THEY WERE MADE. THE YEARS AND THE FILMS ARE:

1977 – Close Encounters of the Third Kind

1982 – ET

1993 – Jurassic Park

FIRST, SIMPLIFY THE NUMBERS.
YOU KNOW THAT ALL
THREE FILMS WERE MADE
IN THE 20TH CENTURY SO
YOU CAN DROP THE 19
AND CONCENTRATE ON THE 77,
82 AND 93 INSTEAD.

NEXT, CONVERT THE YEAR OF THE FIRST FILM INTO ITS
NUMBER–SHAPE. FOR 77 YOU IMAGINE TWO BOOMERANGS.
ENLIVEN THE ASSOCIATION BY USING YOUR IMAGINATION.
IMAGINE THE BOOMERANGS WHIZZING THROUGH THE AIR.
THEN, LINK THE NUMBER–SHAPE TO THE FILM BY
INTEGRATING THE IMAGE INTO ONE OF THE SCENES IN
"CLOSE ENCOUNTERS OF THE THIRD KIND" – PERHAPS
YOU IMAGINE THE PROTAGONIST (PLAYED BY RICHARD
DREYFUSS) THROWING BOOMERANGS INTO THE NIGHT SKY. >

WHAT ABOUT THE NEXT FILM? HOW WOULD YOU VISUALIZE 82 AS NUMBER—SHAPES? ONE WAY WOULD BE TO IMAGINE AN HOURGLASS WITH A SNAKE CURLED AROUND ITS BASE. CONNECT THE IMAGE WITH THE FILM — WHAT WOULD ET MAKE OF THIS IF HE CAME ACROSS IT? PERHAPS HE'D POKE THE SNAKE WITH HIS LONG FINGER.

WHAT ABOUT 93? YOU COULD IMAGINE A BALLOON ON A PIECE OF STRING. FOR A JOKE SOMEONE HAS DRAWN A PAIR OF PUCKERED LIPS ON THE BALLOON. TO LINK THIS WITH JURASSIC PARK YOU COULD IMAGINE THE BALLOON TIED TO THE TAIL OF ONE OF THE DINOSAURS — IT'S MAKING HIM ANGRY!

ALTERNATIVELY, YOU MIGHT IMAGINE THE DINOSAUR WEARING A MONOCLE (AN ALTERNATIVE NUMBER-SHAPE FOR 9) AND PUCKERING HIS OWN LIPS IN READINESS TO KISS A BEAUTIFUL GIRL DINOSAUR HE'S SPOTTED ACROSS THE RIVER.

POSITIVE VISUALIZATION

It's common to imagine yourself drying up mid-way through a speech. This kind of negative visualization fills you with dread and actually impairs your memory. Replace negative images with their exact opposites: imagine giving your audience a huge smile and launching into your speech with confidence and enthusiasm.

THE DOMINIC SYSTEM

If your speech contains a lot of numbers – particularly long numbers – try using my very own DOMINIC system (Decipherment Of Mnemonically Interpreted Numbers Into Characters). It works for every kind of number you can think of – in fact, I have even used it to memorize the Periodic Table and the calendar of the 21st century. ❯

The key to the success of the DOMINIC system is that it links numbers with people who are familiar to you – either famous people or people whom you know personally. In this way, numbers are transformed into familiar faces that are already hard wired into your memory.

For example, which list do you find easiest to remember?

Claudia Schiffer	David Bowie	Clint Eastwood
36	**42**	**35**

I would guess that, if you put the book down, you would still recall the names a minute later, while the figures may have faded.

In fact, the three celebrities represent the three numbers. >

The DOMINIC system works by allocating each number from 0 to 9 a letter. Like this:

0 – O	5 – E
1 – A	6 – S
2 – B	7 – G
3 – C	8 – H
4 – D	9 – N

The rationale for my choice of letters is simple. In the case of 1 to 5, and for 7 and 8, the number is represented by the equivalent letter of the alphabet – 1 to 5 is A to E and 7 and 8 are represented by G and H. For the other numbers, I use the strongest association they have for me. Zero and the letter "O" look similar. Six has two "S" sounds and "nine" has two "N"s. ❯

In order for the DOMINIC system to work, every number from 0 to 99 has to form a pair. So, I put a "0" in front of numbers from 0 to 9 to create 00, 01, 02 and so on. Then, I turn every pair of numbers into a pair of letters. 01 becomes OA, 02 becomes OB ... all the way to 99, which becomes NN.

Next, I think of people who have each of these pairs of letters as their initials. So, for me 23 is Bill Clinton, 42 is David Bowie, and so on. Who would you choose?

Thinking up 100 different people may sound like a tall order, but you can draw people from any number of sources. If no-one famous and no-one you know fits the bill, think of a cartoon or fictional character (for example, Olive Oyl for OO). ❯

When you've got 100 people or characters, you need to commit them to memory. Try to learn 20 a week. In just five weeks you will have memorized a system for remembering numbers that will last you for ever.

As you memorize each person, try to associate them with a specific prop and/or action. This will come in very useful when you need to

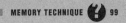

remember numbers that are longer than three digits – you'll see why later on. For example, I associate Eric Clapton (53) with a guitar. For Andre Agassi (11) I make the association of playing tennis and for Olive Oyl (00) I think of her and Popeye eating spinach. ❯

Learning to convert numbers into images is like learning any new skill. At first your brain has to go through each stage methodically, one at a time, because you are making associations that do not come naturally. If you drew a flow chart of your thoughts, it would probably look something like this:

- Look at number
- Convert it into letters

- **Think of letters as initials**
- **Name the person**
- **Create an association that best sums up this person**

However, eventually, your thought processes will become reflexive and converting numbers to people will be instantaneous. Like this:

- **Look at number**
- **Visualize person**

NOW TRY APPLYING THE **DOMINIC** SYSTEM TO LEARNING A SPEECH INVOLVING NUMBERS.

IMAGINE THAT YOU WORK FOR A CHARITY THAT SUPPORTS THE HOMELESS AND YOU ARE GIVING A SPEECH TO A GROUP OF POTENTIAL DONORS. YOUR SPEECH CONTAINS UNWIELDY FIGURES — FROM THE NUMBERS OF YOUNG PEOPLE LIVING ROUGH ON THE STREETS TO THE NUMBER OF HOMES THAT ARE REPOSSESSED ANNUALLY. RATHER THAN REFERRING TO

A PIECE OF PAPER, YOU WANT TO BE ABLE TO REEL OFF THE FIGURES WITHOUT BREAKING EYE CONTACT WITH YOUR AUDIENCE. HERE'S YOUR OPENING GAMBIT:

"THINK WHAT IT WOULD BE LIKE IF YOU DIDN'T HAVE A HOME TO GO BACK TO TONIGHT. 45,300 HOMELESS FAMILIES IN OUR CITY ARE IN EXACTLY THAT POSITION. THIS MEANS 108,700 INDIVIDUAL PEOPLE DON'T HAVE A PERMANENT ROOF OVER THEIR HEAD." >

THESE ARE THE STEPS YOU NEED TO TAKE TO MEMORIZE
THE TWO FIGURES USING THE **DOMINIC** SYSTEM.

1. BREAK DOWN THE NUMBER INTO PAIRS OF DIGITS. IF
THERE IS AN ODD NUMBER OF DIGITS, YOU WILL HAVE ONE
DIGIT LEFT OVER, BUT STEP 3 SHOWS YOU WHAT TO DO.
EACH PAIR OF DIGITS SHOULD BRING A PERSON TO MIND.

2. MEMORIZE THESE PEOPLE IN ORDER BY CREATING A
STORY ABOUT THEM. YOU CAN USE THE PEOPLE OR THEIR
ACTIONS OR PROPS, BUT YOU MUST MAINTAIN THE RIGHT
ORDER OF ASSOCIATIONS. REHEARSE YOUR STORY.

3. IF YOU HAVE A SPARE NUMBER THAT DOES NOT FORM A
PAIR, MEMORIZE THE SINGLE DIGIT THAT YOU HAVE LEFT
OVER USING THE NUMBER–RHYME OR THE NUMBER–SHAPE
SYSTEM. INTEGRATE THIS AT THE END OF YOUR STORY.

How did you get on? This is how I would do it:

Let's take the first figure – 45,300. This becomes 45 and 30 with a 0 left over.

I immediately think of Duke Ellington (DE = 45) and Caroline Oates (CO = 30), a friend of mine who is a keen swimmer. The remaining zero makes me think of a ball (the number–shape for zero). So, if I put all of this together, I imagine Duke Ellington swimming frantically while holding a ball in his hand. You'll notice that I've used the action that I associate with my friend Caroline Oates as a kind of shorthand for her personality. This creates a very economical and easy-to-remember image. It's easier to remember a person performing an action than it is to remember two unrelated people. >

NOW LET'S TAKE THE SECOND FIGURE – 108,700. AS
BEFORE, I BREAK IT DOWN INTO PAIRS OF DIGITS: 10, 87
AND 00. THE PEOPLE WHO REPRESENT THESE FIGURE
PAIRS ARE ANNIE OAKLEY (AO = 10), HUGH GRANT (HG
= 87), WHOM I ASSOCIATE WITH WEDDINGS (BECAUSE OF
THE FILM "FOUR WEDDINGS AND A FUNERAL"), AND
OLIVE OYL (OO = OO). I COMBINE THESE TO CREATE THE

BIZARRE IMAGE OF ANNIE OAKLEY AS A GUEST AT THE
WEDDING OF OLIVE OYL.

AGAIN, I'VE USED THE ACTION THAT I ASSOCIATE WITH
HUGH GRANT TO LINK TWO UNRELATED CHARACTERS.

HAVING CREATED THESE MINI-STORIES FOR MYSELF, I'LL GO
THROUGH THEM IN MY HEAD UNTIL I AM UTTERLY
CONFIDENT ABOUT REMEMBERING THE ORIGINAL NUMBERS.

VISUAL AIDS

Visual aids such as flip charts, transparencies or slides can be fantastically useful when you make a speech. They are not only visually stimulating for the audience but they can act as memory props for you, reminding you where you are in your speech and which points to focus on.

PUTTING IT ALL TOGETHER

When I'm learning a speech I use a combination of techniques. I use a Mind Map to plan my ideas. I use association to make my key words memorable. The Journey Method helps me to remember my key words in the correct order. If my speech contains numbers, I'll use the Number–Rhyme system, the Number–Shape system and/or the DOMINIC system, too.

So, this is how you put it all together. Let's say that you are a company manager and one of your long-standing members of staff (Sally) is leaving to take up a post abroad. You are giving a speech to thank her for her hard work and to say goodbye.

You've made some rough notes about what you want your speech to contain. They go something like this:

MENTION THE DAY THAT SALLY STARTED WORK IN 1994 AND HOW SMALL THE COMPANY WAS THEN (30 EMPLOYEES). EXPLAIN HOW THOSE WERE THE DAYS WHEN EVERYONE HAD TO MUCK IN AND DO EVERYTHING FROM CHANGING THE LIGHTBULBS TO SENDING OUT THE MAIL. SALLY ALWAYS PULLED HER WEIGHT AND WAS ALWAYS IN GOOD SPIRITS — HER CHEERFULNESS AND SENSE OF HUMOUR KEPT EVERYONE GOING. ❯

TODAY THE COMPANY EMPLOYS 150 PEOPLE. SALLY HAS
PLAYED A PIVOTAL ROLE IN SECURING MANY IMPORTANT
CONTRACTS THAT HAVE MADE THE COMPANY SUCCESSFUL —
TALK ABOUT SOME OF THESE IN MORE DETAIL.

MENTION THE CONFERENCE THAT SALLY HELPED TO
ORGANIZE IN ZURICH AND HOW SHE OVERCAME HER FEAR OF
FLYING IN ORDER TO BE ABLE TO ATTEND.

EXPLAIN THAT SALLY IS GOING TO WORK IN ROME AND HOW SHE'S ALREADY BEEN INUNDATED WITH PEOPLE WANTING TO VISIT HER. SAY THAT SHE WILL BE WORKING NEAR TO THE PIAZZALE MICHELANGELO — A FAR CRY FROM THE SCRUFFY OFFICE BLOCK THAT SHE'S IN AT THE MOMENT!

END BY WISHING HER GOODBYE AND GOOD LUCK AND BY SAYING THAT THERE'S ALWAYS A PLACE FOR HER HERE IF SHE GETS TIRED OF ROME.

NOW IT'S TIME TO COMMIT THIS SPEECH TO MEMORY. HAVE A GO YOURSELF BEFORE TURNING THE PAGE TO SEE HOW I WOULD DO IT. >

HOW DID YOU GET ON? HERE'S MY ATTEMPT:

FIRST, I TURN THE NOTES INTO A MIND MAP. THIS WILL HELP TO CONSOLIDATE THE MAIN IDEAS IN THE FORM OF KEY WORDS. MY KEY WORDS ARE: 1994 (SUB-BRANCHES WOULD SHOW 30 EMPLOYEES, MAIL, AND SMILING); PRESENT (SUB-BRANCHES: 150 EMPLOYEES AND ACHIEVEMENTS); ZURICH (SUB-BRANCHES: CONFERENCE AND FLYING); ROME (SUB-BRANCHES: PIAZZALE MICHELANGELO AND GOODBYE).

Next I use association to make my key words more memorable. For example, to remember that Sally will be working near the Piazzale Michelangelo, I think of Michelangelo's statue of David. Some of the associations involve using numbers. For the first key word, I have to remember 1994, while 30 is on one of its sub-branches. I can drop the 19 from 1994, so, using the Dominic system, 94 becomes ND (I think of Neil Diamond), and 30 becomes CO (my friend Caroline Oates). My second key phrase also includes a number — 150 — which has three digits. For this I use the Dominic system and the Number–Shape system — I think of Albert Einstein (15 = AE) jumping through a hoop (the number–shape for zero). ❯

ONCE ALL MY ASSOCIATIONS ARE COMPLETE, I PLACE THEM ALONG THE ROUTE FROM MY HOME TO MY GYM USING THE JOURNEY METHOD. I OPEN MY FRONT DOOR AND IN THE GARDEN I

SEE A HUGE CONCERT STAGE WHERE NEIL DIAMOND IS PERFORMING. MY FRIEND CAROLINE IS SWINGING ON MY GARDEN GATE — THINK OF IT CREAKING UNDER THE STRAIN! THE NEXT STAGE IN MY JOURNEY IS THE BUS

STOP AT THE END OF MY ROAD. I IMAGINE A HUGE POSTER HAS BEEN STUCK THERE SHOWING A BIG, VIBRANT SMILE. ... AND SO ON UNTIL I HAVE MEMORIZED THE WHOLE SPEECH ALONG THE ROUTE.

IF YOU HAVE TO GIVE REGULAR SPEECHES AND PRESENTATIONS, I WOULD RECOMMEND GETTING HOLD OF SOME SAMPLE SPEECHES — TRY SOME OF THE US PRESIDENTIAL SPEECHES THAT ARE AVAILABLE ON THE INTERNET — AND APPLYING THE MEMORY TECHNIQUES THAT YOU HAVE LEARNED IN THIS BOOK. YOUR DELIVERY WILL SOON BECOME SO IMPRESSIVE THAT PEOPLE WILL DEMAND TO KNOW WHAT YOUR SECRETS ARE. AND REMEMBER THAT PRACTICE MAKES PERFECT — THE MORE YOU USE THE TECHNIQUES, THE MORE NATURAL THEY WILL SEEM TO YOU AND THE EASIER IT WILL BE FOR YOU TO MEMORIZE SPEECHES AND PRESENTATIONS IN AN INSTANT.

ACKNOWLEDGMENTS

AUTHOR'S ACKNOWLEDGMENTS

I wish to thank the creative team at Duncan Baird Publishers, including Zoë Stone, Judy Barratt, Bob Saxton and Dan Sturges, for producing this book, and especially Kesta Desmond for her invaluable work.

Editorial Consultant: Kesta Desmond
Managing Editor: Judy Barratt
Editor: Zoë Stone
Managing designer: Dan Sturges
Designer: Adelle Morris
Commissioned Artwork: Maggie Tingle